THE PEOPLE WHO MADE
WELLS
CATHEDRAL
MORE THAN STONE & GLASS

BY SIMON GARRETT & ANNE CRAWFORD

PHOTOGRAPHY PHILIP NASH

FOREWORD

FROM THE DEAN OF WELLS,
THE VERY REVEREND JOHN CLARKE

Wells Cathedral is one of the great buildings of the English landscape. In stone and glass it tells a story that is both local to the county of Somerset and marked by the upheavals of national events. To read this book is to be reminded of the extraordinary characters that have inspired its life and contributed to its construction, as masons and musicians or bishops and deans. The church is a communion of men and women, named and unnamed, saints and sinners, extending through the centuries and across the continents. By attending to the particularity of this special place each person is reminded of their own setting in history. Today visitors come to Wells from many countries, drawn by a beauty in which spirit is closely interwoven with matter. The team that created this book have portrayed by photographs and words a vision that is transcendent and, at the same time, intimate.

LEFT: The Scissor Arches.

INTRODUCTION

What is a cathedral? At its utmost, it is a place of calm, of intense and inclusive spirituality, a haven from the world outside and a place in which to reflect on the world we live in. At its most basic it is a pile of stones and glass but ingeniously and lovingly constructed and dedicated to the worship of God, striving to be worthy of His grace. Least seen but perhaps of most significance, it is a place shaped and constantly redefined by the people who work in it and whose lives are entirely intertwined with its existence. Sometimes a seat of power, sometimes a focus for conflict, it is a witness to history, affecting and being affected by the tides in the affairs of men and thus ever-changing. The word 'cathedral' is derived from the Latin *cathedra* meaning 'seat.' It is literally where the bishop sits; a curiosity today, perhaps, but in times past when the church played such a fundamental role in politics, both global and personal it was a seat of genuine power and authority with enormous influence over king and commoner alike.

Wells is unique. Cathedrals are frequently sited in places considered sacred by pre-Christians. Its location close to the wells worshipped by pagans for centuries is not unusual. What is out of the ordinary is that Wells as a city along with

LEFT: The Nave.

its Somerset hinterland has never been highly populated or a powerful political centre. The great Norman cathedrals of Durham, Norwich or Lincoln were designed as "statements in stone," imposing and awe-inspiring they demonstrated a clear message of the conquerors' indomitable power over the subjugated English population and were paired with equally impressive castles. At Wells no such grandstanding was necessary. The Cathedral's design and construction while no less remarkable or impressive than its cousins has no dual purpose, no requirement for the big political statement. Its beauty is wholly conceived for worship, for spirituality and for approaching the divine through the medium of music.

History comprises the stories of people; their struggles and successes, their fears, hope and dreams. Wells is constructed on the lives of those who have infused it with a *spirit of place* over thirty generations. It has withstood and been moulded by the turbulence of the Black Death, the Reformation, the Civil War, the Monmouth rebellion and the Victorian revival of the Anglican church. This book aims to tell stories of some of those people high and low-born to whose lives it has borne witness. It will try to demonstrate that this Cathedral is built not just of stones and glass, but also of flesh and blood.

ABOVE: Vicars' Close.

LEFT: The Cathedral from the south east.

BEGINNINGS

For as long as there have been people living here, Wells has been a sacred place. The four springs or *welleia*, as they were called in Anglo-Saxon, would have been a holy place over many centuries for pagan worshippers who venerated geographic features like hills, trees or running water. The oldest building yet discovered in the Cathedral precincts is a Romano-British mausoleum or burial chamber whose inhabitants may have been Christians. An 8th century Saxon mortuary chapel was built on top of it at a time when the new religion had become established in England, so much so that Christian missionaries were being dispatched *from* here to find converts in the Frankish Empire, (roughly modern day France and Belgium with parts of Germany and Holland). Not only was it natural that successive centres of spiritual significance should be constructed in the same place it was also part of a clear strategy by the early popes to strengthen the influence of the new church. Issuing instructions around the end of the sixth century Pope Gregory the Great wrote, "The temples of the idols in England should not on any account be destroyed. Augustine must smash the idols, but the temples themselves should be sprinkled with holy water, and altars set up in them in which relics are to be enclosed. For we ought to take advantage of well-built temples by purifying them from

RIGHT: The West Front.

devil-worship and dedicating them to the service of the true God." Gregory was passionate about bringing the English in particular to God, and he recognised that appropriating places of pagan significance for Christianity was a short cut to effective conversion.

In the early eighth century Wells was a "frontier town" in the westward spread of Christianity through the south of England. King Ine of Wessex founded the first church at Wells in about 705, designed specifically as a base from which his priests could go out to attempt to convert the still pagan people of what is now Somerset. Ine seems to have been a sincere rather than opportunist believer and the minster church was dedicated to St. Andrew, a saint of apparent personal importance to him. His most lasting achievement was to formally codify the laws of Wessex in a way not seen before and for much of which Alfred the Great has tended, unfairly, to receive the credit when issuing his own laws a hundred and fifty years later. These laws included fines to be levied on people who did not have their children baptised or neglected to pay their tithes (a tenth of their earnings or produce payable annually to the church). The need to stress these laws in such a way also suggests that Ine faced a degree of resistance from those people he was trying to convert. The early missionaries based at Wells will have had a constant fight to convince local people

LEFT: The Quire showing the bishop's seat or cathedra.

ABOVE: The perpendicular tomb in the chapel of St John the Baptist.

The Chapter House where the business
of the Cathedral was done.

to adopt Christianity. Ine's laws were in part designed to put the weight of the state behind their mission. In his declining years the king decided to put his own spiritual well-being ahead of that of Wessex. Without a clear heir he abdicated the throne in 726 saying he was leaving the job of ruling to "younger men." He travelled to Rome; a pilgrimage which the great chronicler of the time, The Venerable Bede, says was undertaken by surprisingly many people, high and low born, as a visit to the Holy City was thought to increase an individual's chances of being admitted to heaven. The founder of the first church at Wells died in Rome shortly after his arrival.

An institution like a missionary church brings opportunity for those of an entrepreneurial bent, and a thriving local community grew up to provide all the goods and services its priests required. As a response to this local growth in population and the westward spread of Christianity, the existing bishopric of Sherborne was divided up in 909 and Somerset given its own bishop. A bishop needs a seat, and the church at Wells was chosen as his Cathedral. The first incumbent was Athelm, a former monk at Glastonbury. Little is known about Athelm but he must have been a highly effective political animal. Some sixteen or so years after becoming bishop of Wells he was controversially elevated to archbishop of Canterbury. Church law dictated that once a bishop had been given a see (the area for which they are the church's "over-seer") they could not be moved to another; Athelm's promotion rewrote that law. Athelm's ambition appears to have had dynastic

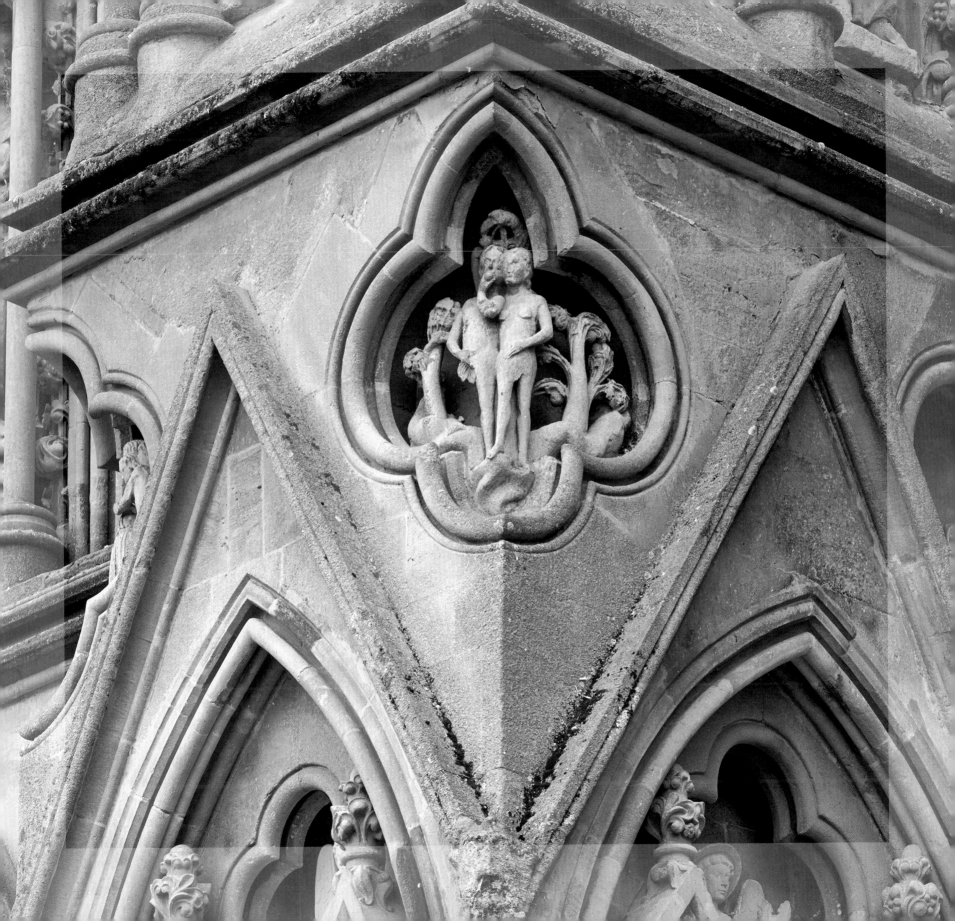

The Cope chest which has held clerical robes for almost 900 years.

qualities. A family member, probably his nephew, was Saint Dunstan, an abbot of Glastonbury who went on to become bishop of Worcester, bishop of London and then archbishop of Canterbury, the most powerful churchman in England.

In 1060, the deeply spiritual King Edward the Confessor appointed the man who was to become the last bishop of the Saxon period, Giso of Lorraine. A great admirer of Norman and continental culture in general, Edward regularly appointed senior churchmen recruited from the other side of the Channel. A tall, impressively built man, Giso was another "big beast" of contemporary politics, and immediately set about superimposing a whole new administrative and religious structure on Wells. When Giso arrived there may have been no more than four or five clergy on the staff. The church had never been a monastic institution and these were secular canons, that is to say, priests whose work was out in the world. Giso must have stirred some resentment, especially among the older canons, when he imposed new fangled foreign ideas upon them. They were reorganised into a semi-monastic way of life more familiar to their continental equivalents. However, the ever energetic bishop also brought significant practical improvement building them a dormitory, refectory and cloister. He obtained grants of land from the king enabling them to support themselves where previously they had been reduced to begging for bread. In so doing, Giso ruffled the very important feathers of Harold Godwinson, earl of Wessex. Godwinson's sister was the king's wife; he was the most powerful man in England after the king and was greatly suspicious of Norman influences. The oldest document in the Cathedral archives is a letter from the pope, Nicholas II, confirming Giso's rights to the estates and other possessions of the bishopric, property greatly coveted by Harold. When the earl seized the throne on Edward's death, Giso's position must have become potentially perilous. How delighted and relieved he must have been at the new king's defeat at the battle of Hastings in 1066, and the arrival of the Norman Conqueror William.

Giso's successor, John of Tours, was probably even less popular with the canons than his predecessor had been. Top jobs in the church were often given as reward to people who had done the king useful service. Giso had been Edward the Confessor's private chaplain. John was William the Conqueror's personal physician. John clearly had a convincing bedside manner even though he lacked much by way of "book learning." A well known contemporary and scholar, William of Malmesbury, said John's mode of speech was so "artless" that when he did speak even children laughed at him. His other best known personal attribute was that he liked a drink, frequently and in some volume. William II, the Conqueror's son, gave him Wells in recognition of his service to his father. John also acquired the wealthy abbey at Bath to help enrich his bishopric. Wells was a small, relatively poor rural community; by contrast Bath was an important enough town to host the coronation of Edgar, the first King of all England in 973, and it even boasted its own mint. John decided to "go where the money

RIGHT: The Giso letter of 1060 is still held in the Cathedral archives.

ABOVE: Detail of the Papal Seal drawn on the Giso letter of 1060.

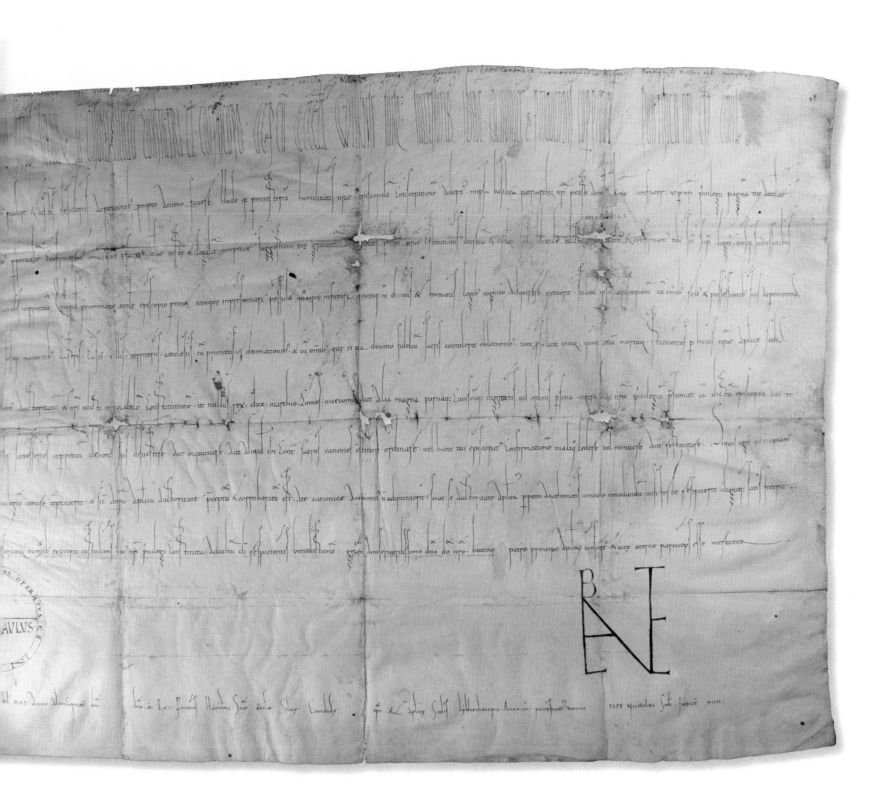

was" and promptly moved the see or seat of his bishopric there in 1088, building a new Norman-style priory, and leaving Wells to become a humble college of canons whose income and prestige were significantly reduced as a result. Thus it remained an economic and spiritual backwater for almost a hundred years.

The saviour of Wells was Bishop Reginald de Bohun (pronounced Boon), a successful diplomat and a close relation to the French royal family and a fan of hawking and hunting with dogs. He was closely involved in what was the most violent and traumatic rift between church and state since Christianity had been established in England. Before becoming bishop Reginald worked as an expert in church law for the archbishop of Canterbury, Thomas Becket. A celebrated soldier, administrator and politician, Becket was King Henry II's right hand man and became archbishop of Canterbury. However, the two men had a tumultuous falling out and Becket was exiled, during which time he excommunicated or threw out of the church, a number of his enemies including Reginald's own father. In 1169, Reginald's lawyer's skills were called upon as he accompanied Henry to Montmirail near Chartres to take part in talks aimed at reconciling Becket and the French king. When the conference collapsed in yet more rage and recrimination, Becket excommunicated a further collection of his enemies, including Reginald.

RIGHT: Bishop Giso's mortuary cross.

FAR RIGHT: The effigy of Bishop Giso was found to contain his remains.

RIGHT: The heavily modified stone font was brought to the "new" Gothic Cathedral from the "old" Saxon building.

LEFT: The lead name plate found with Bishop Giso's remains.

In 1170 Becket, having returned to England no less determined than ever to stand up to the king, was notoriously murdered in his own Cathedral at the hands of four of Henry's knights. Reginald who had closely served both men became bishop three years later.

In 1175, Reginald started work on rebuilding the church at Wells. Possibly for ease of construction, the new building was slightly to the north of the Anglo-Saxon Cathedral, the remains of which lie beneath its cloisters. Wells was to be built in the new Gothic style. No more thick walls, rounded arches and massive pillars of the Norman tradition. Instead pointed arches, slender pillars, and higher walls with elaborate ceiling vaulting would be employed, allowing for better light through larger windows and therefore more room for stained glass. Wells was the first English cathedral to be completely built in this new style. It is amusing to speculate that as with most new directions in architecture, many may have tutted under their breath as the structure grew, shaking their heads at such an "ugly modern building." In November 1191 Reginald was named as the new archbishop of Canterbury but his enemies launched appeals against his election. A few weeks later and before those appeals could be heard, he died without being confirmed in the highest office of the English Church.

Reginald's successor tended to be otherwise engaged when it came to the new Cathedral. Savaric fitzGeldewin is thought to have been a second cousin of Reginald's as he was of the Holy Roman Emperor, Henry VI. While he came with Reginald's recommendation his election was more than a little controversial. A close friend of Richard I (the Lionheart), he was put in post while

away on Crusade with the King in Sicily. Richard had given him letters effectively promising him the next English bishopric which fell vacant. The king would later claim Savaric somehow forced him into writing them, but the possibility of a bribe passing between them was also rumoured at the time. The canons felt they had been railroaded but were left with little choice but to accept. Savaric's election was duly confirmed in December 1191. Savaric was previously archdeacon of Northampton and of Salisbury but it was not until nine months later that he was ordained as a priest in Rome and consecrated as bishop the next day – a meteoric rise indeed. He then departed with the king on the disastrous Third Crusade. When Savaric was not "fighting for Christendom," he was involved in a lengthy struggle to absorb the wealthy and prestigious monastery of Glastonbury into his see for financial rather than spiritual reasons. When the abbot of Glastonbury went to Rome to fight his corner and unexpectedly died, there were dark rumours that he had been poisoned either by Savaric or under his orders. His swashbuckling career would later involve attempting to negotiate the Lionheart's ransom from captivity in Germany, being held there as a hostage himself and being named Imperial Chancellor of Burgundy. Savaric died in 1205, not in Wells, nor in Bath, nor even in Burgundy, but in Italy where he was attempting to have confirmed the election of the new bishop of Winchester to whom he owed a favour. In spite of Savaric's preoccupation with affairs away from Wells building work had continued during his term of office. The Quire (literally the area for the choir) was completed in about 1200 and the remains of seven Saxon bishops (including Giso) brought across from the previous building. Their effigies can still be seen today laid upon modern (c. 1914) tomb chests but still holding the bones they were built to contain. These were examined in 1979 and six of them were found to be accompanied by rather helpful lead nameplates.

Having been of little apparent consequence to Savaric, Wells was clearly of singular importance to the man who followed him as bishop. Bishop Jocelin was already a canon of Wells at the time of his consecration and is strongly believed to have been born in the city. He had already worked for the crown, Reginald and for Savaric. His tenure did not start well. The new king John, Richard the Lionheart's brother, had refused to accept the Pope's nomination of Stephen Langton as archbishop of Canterbury. As a result, the

whole country was placed under a papal interdict in 1208, meaning while nobody was actually excommunicated, they could no longer receive the sacraments or act as priests. Jocelin was one of many caught between Church and State and chose to go into exile, not returning until 1213 when the king restored his position and estates as part of the settlement with the pope. The power struggle over Glastonbury continued for another five years, but Jocelin negotiated a settlement which would have lasting positive repercussions for Wells. Part of the deal involved the bishop being given a number of highly profitable manors which had been under the monks' control. It was the money raised from the proceeds of these lands which Jocelin poured into the continuing construction of the Cathedral. This work included putting the roof on the Nave (the main body of the building) and creating the West Front and culminated in the Cathedral being dedicated to Saint Andrew in 1239. During Jocelin's time in exile he seems to have bought himself a beautiful Limoges enamel crosier (bishop's ceremonial staff) which can be seen along with his ring in the Cathedral library, both of which were found in his tomb.

BUILDERS

Building cathedrals in the days before mechanical diggers, cranes and power tools was a slow process. By most standards Wells was constructed remarkably quickly, in perhaps a little more than fifty years. The building brought to life by Jocelin was to all intents and purposes identical in its design and dimensions to that first mapped out in Reginald's de Bohun's time. Much of the credit for this consistency must go to the master masons of the Cathedral, the men who saw it as their duty to realise the original vision of the first plans. Like the bishops they served, one succeeding the other, so they took up the work where death or infirmity had robbed the project of their predecessor. The job combined architect, project manager and site foreman, and for each master mason it was the task of a lifetime, all knowing that only the last of their line would live to see their work completed. The name of the first of these remarkable craftsmen is unknown. He was responsible for the building of the Quire and probably began the construction of the Transepts (the arms of the building which cross the nave at right angles). The identity of his successor is known. Adam Lock took charge of the works in about 1213 and dedicated the next sixteen years to them, right up until his death. The numbers of men available to Lock and to the other masters would have varied over time, depending on how much money the current bishop was willing or able to commit to the project. However it is likely hundreds were involved in times of peak productivity, ranging from labourers fetching and carrying

RIGHT: The Four Maries.

through craftsmen like carpenters and the highly skilled stone masons who created the beautiful carvings and statuary which still adorn the building today. One can imagine Lock and the other masters planning the use of their workers over the short and long term, manoeuvring them like chess pieces to make sure the work was done and remained on budget. Lock was probably responsible for the North Porch and most of the Nave and was during his lifetime almost certainly the most important layman in the city. Certainly his responsibility would have been reflected in wealth and status. This is best illustrated by the fact that at his death in 1229, only ten years before the dedication of the Cathedral, his widow Agnes and son Thomas sold land and several houses in the area. At the western end of the Nave, high up on the wall, there is a carving of a man in a mason's cap, which has long been believed to be a representation of Lock himself.

If Lock and his unknown predecessor take the credit for the great scope of this enormous and ambitious building, it is his successor who was fortunate to oversee the Cathedral's great glory, the West Front, with its nearly three hundred statues. His name was Thomas Norris and he is responsible for the largest outdoor sculpture gallery in Europe. Norris clearly appreciated the impact his facade would have when first seen by a new visitor. Where now it is all the uniform, if rather lovely, golden colour of the local Doulting stone from which it is constructed, it was once a blaze of bright colour, reds and

LEFT: The Nave.

ABOVE: Is this the face of master mason Adam Lock?

blues and golds. Only tiny patches of this exultant paintwork remain, the rest having been worn away by eight centuries of sun, wind and rain, but in its time it must have seemed like a vision of heaven itself, a dazzling backdrop to the religious processions which made their way across the green. The statues themselves are mostly biblical, saintly or royal. Most are men but notable among the women are Eve from the Garden of Eden, the Queen of Sheba and, round the corner of the North West tower, facing the North Porch and on the lowest tier, two pairs of figures known as the Four Maries. Only two of the figures can be firmly identified by their attributes: the second from the nave wall is Mary Magdalene, carrying her pot of ointment, and the fourth, closest to the road, is almost certainly the Virgin Mary because she is wearing a chasuble, a priestly garment forbidden to all other women. Despite the persistence of the Four Maries label, the two other figures cannot be identified; they might perhaps be Anne, mother of the Virgin or Elizabeth, mother of John the Baptist. Imagine the sense of responsibility and the excitement of the masons given the task of producing these beautiful figures. How intense in a time of universally accepted religious belief must it have been to take up one's tools

LEFT: A canon holding a scroll on the North Porch.

RIGHT The Chapter House.

and create a representation of the Mother of God? How satisfying to know that that creation might stand, inspiring awe in all who view it, for centuries after the craftsman's death?

What a job it must have been for those craftsmen to be involved with. A cursory glance at the images they created shows just how much freedom they were given and how much they allowed their imaginations to run riot. The 13th century capitals of Wells (the top part of the pillars) are unique. There is nothing quite like them anywhere else. The carvings of typically English foliage are enlivened by a large variety of men, animals, birds and mythical creatures peering out from the leaves. There are no two the same and because Wells is not a particularly large cathedral and does not have the soaring columns and high roof of many others, the capitals can be seen clearly from the ground. Some tell a story, like that of the martyrdom of St. Edmund in the North Porch (beheaded by Vikings, a wolf retrieved Edmund's missing head,

returning it to his servants to be reunited with his body so he might be whole for the Day of Resurrection), but most of the carvings are not of religious subjects. The most famous is in the South Transept, where the four sides of the capital nearest the exit to the East Cloister show the story of the Grape Stealers. The first side shows the two thieves at work, the next, the farmer's man pointing them out to his master, the third sees the thief grabbed by the ear and then in the last he is beaten by the farmer. Everywhere there is humour almost verging on the irreverent. For the people who came to worship at Wells it must have been a treat. Books were very scarce and the vast majority of the population could not read so they were taught through pictures. A visit to the Cathedral will have inspired wonder and awe, certainly, but it would also have been a source of good old-fashioned fun.

A quick glance at many of the figures carved inside the Cathedral puts paid to ideas we may have of medieval religion being entirely about piety and seriousness. It seems at every turn, in every corner, there lurks yet another grisly, grotesque or gleeful character. There are no fewer than eleven carvings of men with toothache, nine of them in the transepts; one of the best is on the north wall of the Nave, near the present virgers' office, where with a ladder and a torch it is possible to see right into the sufferer's mouth, where his tongue is pressed agonisingly against his aching tooth.

Carvings could also be functional. On the south wall of the Nave are two large heads of a king and a bishop. Here are the

The story of the Grape Stealers.

twin pillars and powers of medieval society, church and state. Their job was to support the Cathedral's earliest known organ, not much bigger than a modern piano, set up on high about 1310. It might seem odd to us that the organ would have been stuck half way up a wall, but while it may have helped with the acoustics the spiritual reasoning is clear. The music of Wells was for the glory of God, and surely, by being higher up, it would be easier for Him to hear.

In the quire, Wells has one of the finest sets of misericords in the country. These are the hinged seats in each of the canons' stalls where they could prop themselves up during services while still looking as if they were standing. This might sound like cheating or laziness, but when one appreciates that there were eight services every day it becomes understandable. There are sixty-four seats in all, (although only one or two can be displayed), created in oak in the 1330s. Each consists of a figure, either animal or human, between roundels of foliage. The animals are wonderfully lifelike and include mythical dragons and monsters. There are fewer humans, none are biblical images, and only one, the head of a bishop, is religious. This is another example of the way the craftsmen involved took every opportunity to showcase their talents,

are not the only concession to comfort. Around the walls of the nave there are banks of low stone seating. These were specifically for the ease of the old or sick or of nursing mothers and their existence gave rise to the expression, "the weakest go to the wall." Today they even have radiators beneath them and have always been a favourite haunt of Louis, the celebrated Cathedral cat.

As with the West Front, the interior of the building would have been a blaze of colour. Wall paintings showed saints and stories, educating and entertaining the public who only worshipped here on saints' days and festivals. Brightly painted statues, priestly vestments and altar cloths added to the spectacle. While the weather is to blame for the loss of colour outside, it was the newly installed Protestant authorities during the Reformation in the sixteenth century who whitewashed the painted interior (of which more later). For a clue regarding what it must have been like, we can look at the two tombs in the South Transept, where considerable amounts of paint remain. The nave roof was originally painted in the thirteenth century. It was repainted in 1845 and 1985 but follows the original medieval pattern. The earliest pieces of stained glass date from about 1290 and can be seen

probably inspired by each other's work; carpenters competing with masons and glass makers all vying to produce the most beautiful or elaborate creations. They carved or painted mythical creatures from their imagination like dragons or griffins (half lion, half eagle). They made creatures from the countryside around them, like the delightful birds, interspersed with daisies, in the west window of St Katherine's Chapel, which date from the 15th century, or the dog with a bone in the lavabo (a basin for hand washing) at the entrance to the Undercroft. Yet more exotic creatures like lions which they had probably never seen were copied from bestiaries (books of animal drawings). The misericords

The North Porch.

above the Chapter House steps. The finest is the magnificent east window above the Quire. The Jesse, or Golden Window, subject of a major restoration in 2011-2013, is a lesson in scripture. Installed around 1340, it shows the central story of the birth, death and resurrection of Jesus, surrounded by some of his earthly ancestors going back to Abraham in the form of a vine springing from the side of Jesse, father of King David. Above Jesse is a delightful image of the Virgin and Child and at the very top, Christ in Glory.

All over the Cathedral are series of regular marks scratched into smooth stone surfaces, not graffiti (though we have many examples of that, too), but the individual signs of medieval masons. These are like an artist's signature on a painting, the masons quite literally leaving their mark. By identifying a specific craftsman's work, travelling masons, not on the permanent staff, could have the quality of their work checked. If they were doing piece work, their progress could be marked at the beginning and end of each day. Similarly, when the master mason or his deputy picked out particular stones at the quarry these would also be marked. These "signatures" help architectural historians to calculate roughly how many

A misericord; blessed relief for long-standing canons.

masons were at work on any particular part of the building. In the lower part of the Central Tower, to take one example, a total of fifteen different marks have been found, of whom two had worked on the Transepts and the eastern end of the Nave. Five others also work on the east Nave, four of whom continued on its west and eight apparently did no other work in the Cathedral. Some of the marks appear upside down and others in positions where it would have been impossible to carve them in situ so have to have been made in the masons' yard, before the stone was set in place.

Even though the Cathedral was dedicated in 1239 work did not stop there and certainly the 21st century has seen a significant amount of change. Fashionable cloisters were added on the south side in the mid 13th century, forming an enclosed cloister garth (a courtyard or garden) known as the Palm Churchyard. Once the church of St Andrew had again become a cathedral, the administration needed somewhere to conduct its affairs. The Dean and Chapter is the name used for the governing body of the Cathedral. The Chapter in the Middle Ages comprised all the canons, up to fifty in number, who elected the dean as their chairman. The Chapter House, with

its impressive Undercroft (a vaulted room beneath it), now the Interpretation Centre, was completed in 1306. Here the Chapter conducted their daily business, often involving the running of their landed estates and therefore their income. They also dealt with any disciplinary measures necessary against canons or vicars choral. Before the Reformation a great many of the cases were to do with bad behaviour of a carnal kind. One vicar when accused of keeping a concubine claimed in his defence that all the vicars had mistresses. This may have been a bit of an exaggeration but a number of vicars were clearly less than chaste. For example in 1493, a vicar and chantry priest called Simon Lane admitted committing adultery with the daughter of a local burgess. As a penance he was ordered to go before the procession in the Cathedral on the following Sunday with a wax taper he was to offer at the image of St Andrew. He was suspended from wearing his habit or receiving his pay for six months. This was a particularly harsh punishment and may have been as a result of a complaint from the girl's father. Each canon had his stall ranged round the walls of the Chapter House, while his vicar or deputy sat on the lower row of seats below. Vicars, stewards, bailiffs or tenants waiting to be called in sat on the stone benches below the windows of the great staircase. In the vestibule at the entrance to the Chapter House sat an official to guard the privacy of the meeting. The "doorkeeper" might have to sit for hours keeping watch, especially on days when the Chapter was in session as an ecclesiastical court, with witnesses sitting on the seats by the steps.

LEFT: Church & State, a bishop and a king supported the original organ.

INSET: Medieval business card, a mason's mark.

On the stone bench on the left hand side of the vestibule is an inserted stone with a board game scratched on it; presumably put there to alleviate the boredom of hours of tedious waiting. The Chapter House is now only used for ceremonial purposes, being rather large and chilly for modern ideas of comfort, but when it was in use, what political rows, infighting and jostling for power must have gone on there?

The cloisters and the Chapter House were physically joined to the church but not part of it. Inside the sacred space a new Lady Chapel was built during the first quarter of the 14th century, replacing an earlier one quite separate from the main body of the church. Then the Quire was extended eastwards to meet it, with the space known as the Retroquire (the area behind the altar) joining the two. At the same time it was decided to raise the Central Tower. This had unforeseen consequences which could have spelt disaster. It was quickly realised that extra weight of the taller tower was too much for the pillars of the crossing to bear, and they sank some three or four inches from the strain. Large cracks appeared in the tower and it was clear something had to be done. The Scissor Arches (or St Andrew's Arches as they are sometimes known) look almost as if they were built yesterday. In fact they were one of the measures taken in the 14th century to stop the Cathedral collapsing under its own weight. Internal buttresses were put in and high up on both sides of the crossing, windows were partially blocked for added support and yet more buttressing, clearly visible from both transepts and also in the first nave bay. These probably did most of the work in stabilising the structure, redistributing the stresses and halting the collapse of the tower. However, the Cathedral authorities must still have been unconvinced. Thomas of Whitney, master mason at the start of the proceedings, was succeeded by William Joy. He installed the Scissor Arches between 1338 and 1348 in a final effort to save the tower. Modern experts tell us the buttresses had already taken the weight successfully and that the Scissor Arches were probably unnecessary. Certainly there has been no further subsidence since they were built. Even so, one cannot help but have sympathy for church administrators, listening to Joy's dire warnings of impending collapse if they did not find the funds

ABOVE LEFT: St Mark and his lion.

RIGHT: Painted details from the tomb of Bishop William of March.

necessary to pay for his load-bearing arches. After all, who would want to go down in history as the bishop or dean who allowed Wells Cathedral to fall in a heap? Either way, Joy's legacy is a piece of architecture which makes the view up the Nave at Wells instantly recognisable.

With such huge ongoing building costs, cathedrals always were, and are, strapped for cash. As a result much of the building work had to be funded by the bishops from their own pockets, sometimes with the help of donations from pious laymen. Thereafter the Cathedral authorities had to pay for upkeep. The problem was especially acute at Wells. Cathedrals raised money from pilgrims and tourists coming to see their shrines to significant local saints or holy relics like saints' bones or pieces of the cross on which Christ was crucified. Such relics as Wells had were insufficient to attract pilgrims. Various fund raising schemes were considered. There were attempts to foster a cult around Bishop William of March [1292-1302], even twice proposing him for canonisation in the hope that they could build a shrine for him in the new Retroquire, behind the high altar. This was surely a sign of desperation. Candidates for canonisation have to be credited with miracles; Bishop William was reputedly very pious but that was about it and the application was rejected. The consolation prize for his supporters was a very fine painted stone tomb (easily mistaken for wood) in the South Transept which hides an unusual secret. At the top of it is an opening beneath which is a small, hidden room. This appears to be almost a shrine-

LEFT: Leading to the Chapter House and known as the Sea of Steps.

BELOW: The door-keeper's gaming board.

in-waiting, as it was found to contain relics and some of his clothes. Such open reliquaries are extremely unusual, and, as William was never made a saint, in this case, unused. A much more promising candidate for canonisation would have been Bishop William Bitton [1267-1274], nephew of an earlier bishop of the same name. He was particularly pious, made his mark in his diocese rather than on the national stage, donated estates to the Cathedral and insisted on maintaining a high standard of singing among the vicars and choristers. A case could also have been made for miracles it seems, as for the remainder of the Middle Ages, prayers to him were believed to be particularly effective in remedying toothache, and offerings at his tomb were greater than anywhere else except those for the Virgin Mary.

ABOVE: A medieval pun, the hares on Bishop Harewell's tomb.

RIGHT: The Bell Tower.

The 14th century Bishop Harewell [1366 – 1386] takes much of the credit for the Cathedral's bells. In the Middle Ages, bells were first hung in the lower part of the Central Tower and the clock bell was still there until recently. Harewell gave two thirds of the cost of building the South West Tower and gave a new tenor bell, known as Great Harewell, one of the heaviest anywhere at 56 cwts. (2845 kilos), and another called Little Harewell. The present tenor bell still bears his name. It has been recast several times and some of the metal from Little Harewell was used to strengthen it. By 1415 all the ringing bells had been moved to the new tower giving Wells the heaviest ring of ten bells in the world. Bishop Harewell's tomb is in the South Quire Aisle; his alabaster effigy is covered with 17th and 18th century graffiti. It was originally painted and traces of red can still be seen in the folds of his cloak. Today, the bell ringers of the Cathedral, members of the Wells Amateur Bellringing Society, are by far the noisiest of its hundreds of volunteers, but the bells themselves are pretty inaccessible and so rarely seen by visitors.

GLORY

The two centuries between the mid 14th century and the Reformation were among the most glorious in the history of the Cathedral. The purpose of the Cathedral and its canons in the Middle Ages was to serve God by singing the eight services or canonical hours each day and celebrate frequent masses. There were on average forty-fifty canons of the Cathedral, but only about a dozen of those were resident in Wells at any one time. Each canon therefore, had a "vicar" (from the Latin *vice* meaning deputy) to sing the services in their place. These vicars choral, now the men of the choir, together with boy choristers, have been singing their songs of praise from the original Cathedral's very foundation. In 1348 Bishop Ralph of Shrewsbury founded the College of Vicars Choral and provided them with a communal hall and forty-two individual houses round a quadrangle, now known as Vicars' Close. A little later a chapel was built at the north end and an office wing added to the hall from where the vicars administered the estates which funded the college. It still houses a glorious medieval filing cabinet. This wing was closed in the late nineteenth century and left untouched ever since although it is open to the public once a year. The Close is the only complete medieval street in England. Although the provision of gardens, modern windows and the doubling up of the original houses to provide family homes has altered its appearance no building is later than the 15th century. The

LEFT: The painted tomb of Bishop William of March.

ABOVE: Windows blocked when the Scissor Arches were built.

vicars and other members of the Cathedral foundation still live there. If the visitor stands in the Close and looks up towards the first floor window of the office it is easy to see why it was placed there. The clerk whose room it was was an employee, certainly, but from such a vantage point he would have been well able to observe the comings and goings of the residents, keeping a keen eye on their behaviour.

Ralph's interventions greatly improved the lot of the vicars choral including actively encouraging them to take study leave to improve their education. He is also credited with giving fresh impetus to the building work, but he very nearly did not have the chance to take up his office. Ralph was a canon at Wells in his own right, a doctor of theology, keeper of the king's wardrobe and chancellor of Oxford University, but when the bishopric became vacant the pope had other ideas about who should get the job. The pope was furious with his appointment and letters supporting Ralph from his two chapters at Bath and at Wells, from Oxford and from a host of other notables did nothing to appease him. What did work was cold, hard cash. Ralph is known to have offered the pope two thousand florins in 1330, a very large bribe, and clearly spent a great deal over time gaining His Holiness's approval. This is not to say that he was devoid of piety or commitment to the church. According to the Oxford Dictionary of National Biography, "Historians have regarded him as an exemplary medieval bishop and in his lifetime he gained a reputation for

ABOVE: Canon Hugh Sugar's coat of arms on the chimneys.

RIGHT: Vicars' Close.

The steward's room.

RIGHT: The steward's room with a view down the medieval Vicars' Close.

sanctity." Certainly he could not be accused of being an absentee bishop, spending the vast majority of the rest of his life within the diocese of Wells. During the Black Death, the period when plague is estimated to have killed up to a third of the population of Europe, unable to mend their bodies his thoughts were for victims' souls. He set up emergency regulations for the sick to make their final confessions to lay people if there were no clergy available. While not put forward for sainthood, there is evidence that his tomb was particularly visited by members of the public up to thirty years after his death.

At any given time there would be about six boy choristers living together under the supervision of the Master of the Choristers. Bishop Ralph built them a house in 1354, the remains of which now form the staircase wall of the Chapter Two restaurant. Many went on to become vicars choral but even if they did not, they had received the benefit of a good education. From the 15th century they were taught in a schoolroom newly built over the West Cloister; today they attend the Cathedral School. The Cathedral was a busy place. The vicars choral and the choristers sang the main services in the quire each day. It is important to understand that these were not services being held for the public and generally there would have been nobody but the clergy and choristers present. Their purpose was to sing and hold services for the glory of God. The words and music were for His benefit alone. There were other altars around the building where masses were

also constantly being celebrated. With so many services following each other they had to run to a strict schedule. To that end, some time shortly before 1392 the famous Wells clock was installed. Its medieval mechanism is now in the Science Museum in London, but everything else, the complex dial, the jousting horsemen and the figure of Jack Blandifer striking his bell to mark the passage of time dates from the late fourteenth century. Nobody knows who Jack Blandifer was or why he was chosen for his role. He is medieval but a later repair and repainting has given him a distinctly 17th century look. The clock face next to which he sits is believed to be the oldest surviving clock face in the world.

The masses the clock regulated were often only attended by the celebrant. While members of the public would have been able to be present they were few in number. These services were largely paid for by pious townsfolk, often so that in return prayers would be said for the dead of their family to help

ABOVE TOP: Bishop Bekynton's tomb.

ABOVE: The jester in Bekynton's chantry.

RIGHT: Bishop Bubwith's chantry.

speed their progress through Purgatory. Money could be left for just one service a year on the anniversary of the death, or more frequently, depending on the amount of money given. The wealthiest men, usually the bishops, were able to fund a separate chapel (called a chantry), with its own dedicated priest, specifically to say prayers for their souls. One such, on the north side of the nave is that of Nicholas Bubwith, who died in 1424. Bubwith was a serial bishop having previously held the posts in London and Salisbury before becoming bishop of Bath and Wells in 1407. He had already been Henry IV's secretary, lord privy seal and treasurer of England. Such was his wealth that when he died not only did he leave sufficient funds to pay for the chapel but for four priests to serve it saying prayers for his soul. He also bequeathed money to build the Cathedral Library. The idea of prayers for the dead was considered blasphemous to the zealots of the Reformation and everywhere Cathedral authorities were ordered to abolish chantries and their chapels. Luckily, Bubwith's chapel was in such a place that much damage would have been done to the fabric of the Cathedral if it had been removed so it was left alone. Instead it was used for storing wood. On its wall can still be seen Bubwith's coat of arms comprising three holly wreaths which are also present in the stained glass windows of the Library.

Unlike many cathedrals, Wells does not house the tombs of kings or prominent laymen. Its grandest tombs all belong to bishops and the occasional dean. The most striking of all is that of Bishop Thomas Bekynton. Fifteen years before

THIS PAGE:
Bishop Bekynton's
serene effigy.

RIGHT: Vicars' Hall

his death in 1465, the bishop had his own chantry chapel on the south side of the quire prepared for his tomb. This is a striking double-decker, with the bishop, beaming cherubically in his robes above and a decaying body below, a reminder that death comes to all no matter how important. Not easily seen is the figure of the bishop's jester on the side of the tomb facing the high altar (a private joke of the bishop's perhaps). When his

grave was opened he was found to have been buried with humble simplicity. Bekynton, a Somerset man, was the last of the great building bishops. To him Wells owes the four great gateways around Cathedral Green, the most impressive of which is the Chain Gate, linking Vicars' Hall to the top of the stairs to the Chapter House at first floor level. This bridge spans what was for centuries the main road to Bath, and allowed the vicars to move easily from their hall into the Cathedral for services without suffering rain, wind or snow. The addition of the outside face of the Cathedral clock, which can be seen from the hall, left no excuses for bad time-keeping. Bekynton's gift to the citizens of Wells was a water supply laid from the wells in the palace grounds to the Market Place. Bekynton had been an enormous influence over the young king Henry VI and had been lord privy seal as well as ambassador to France. His lifelong passion was education and he gave generously to Winchester School and Lincoln College, Oxford, as well as drawing up the legal paperwork for Henry to found Eton College.

Some of Wells' finest tombs from this period are tantalisingly mysterious. The one in St Calixtus' Chapel is dated to about 1450 and often ascribed, probably wrongly, to Thomas Boleyn (precentor of Wells 1451-72). It has some very fine alabaster carving - a technique for which English craftsmen were famed in the 15th century. The Annunciation scene at the east end is one of the finest examples of its kind. It has a delicate Virgin with lilies in the foreground. In the centre are three canons, mourning, and their clothes are often taken as a good example of the vestments worn at the time. At the west end is a representation of the Holy Trinity. God the Father cradles his crucified Son and there are three holes in the top right-hand corner, where a dove, the Holy Spirit, may have once been attached. Other noted alabaster carvings are the effigies on the tombs of bishops Harewell and Bekynton.

At the right of the Lady Chapel, dividing it from the chapel of John the Baptist, is a tomb with a lofty canopy, some of the best perpendicular architecture (that is emphasising strong vertical lines) in the Cathedral and dating from the early 14th century. Its size and position suggests that it was designed for an important cleric, but who that was has never been identified.

More often than not in the history of the construction and development of the Cathedral it is the bishops who get the glory. However, one outstanding dean cannot be ignored. Historically, the dean was responsible for the everyday running of the Cathedral. John Gunthorpe was given the job in 1472 as a reward for services rendered to the king. He was a scholar and diplomat at the time of the Renaissance when there was a dramatic explosion of interest in the ancient world and the spread of learning across Europe was greatly helped by the recent invention of printing. He travelled widely and while in Venice in 1472, just before he came to Wells, bought a copy of Pliny's *Natural History*, effectively the first

LEFT: Keeping time at Wells for more than six hundred years.

ABOVE: Jack Blandifer.

RIGHT: Bishop Bubwith's holly wreaths.

Roman encyclopaedia. The book was lost to Wells during the upheaval of the Reformation. Incredibly, one of Gunthorpe's successors as dean found it in an Oxford bookshop two hundred years later, and recognising Gunthorpe's name written inside it, bought it and returned it to the Library. Gunthorpe was responsible for building what is now the oldest part of the Old Deanery.

Formerly a servant of Richard III he entertained his Tudor successor Henry VII, there in 1487. Gunthorpe's boss, Bishop Robert Stillington, was at the time languishing in jail. Stillington had been instrumental in Richard III's seizure of the throne. He told Richard, then duke of Gloucester, that the marriage of Edward IV and Elizabeth Woodville had been invalid because Edward had already been betrothed to Lady Eleanor Talbot. This conveniently meant the royal children were illegitimate and gave Richard the excuse he needed to take the throne. When Richard was killed at the battle of Bosworth in 1485 and Henry VII crowned king, Stillington was thrown in jail. Such was Henry's annoyance with Stillington that his arrest warrant was actually issued on the same day and immediately after the end of the battle. Stillington's prison term seems not to have taught him much by way of caution. In 1487 he threw his weight behind the Lambert Simnel rebellion, where a baker's son was put forward in a half-baked plot by Henry's enemies pretending to be the young earl of Warwick, Richard III's nephew and a claimant to the throne who was actually in prison. This time there would be no second chance. When the rebel army was routed, Stillington fled to Oxford University but was eventually handed over to the king and died in prison. In the absence of episcopal control Gunthorpe kept his steady hand on the tiller until his death in 1498. His painted tomb is in St Katherine's Chapel, but there is no effigy.

The medieval mind took much pleasure in visual puns. Not content with erecting their coats of arms, a number of senior clergy delighted in using a badge which was a play on their name, known as a rebus. Bishop Bekynton created a rebus which showed a beacon and a tun or large barrel. Canon Hugh Sugar's chantry, dated 1489, on the south side of the nave altar, has several badges showing sugar loaves or cones (the way in which sugar was then sold). Thomas Cornish, d. 1513, who was the first suffragan,

ABOVE: Fragments of glass in the Lady Chapel.

RIGHT: The Lady Chapel.

The Chain Library.

or assistant bishop, uses badges with sheaves of corn on his tomb on the wall next to the door leading from the North Transept to the Chapter House. Bishop Harewell does not use a badge, but at the feet of his alabaster effigy in the south quire aisle lie two hares, drinking water bubbling from a well.

In the early sixteenth century Wells succumbed to a little continental influence. An Italian bishop, Hadrian de Castello, held the see from 1504-1518. He arrived in England in 1489 as the collector of "Peter's Pence," effectively a tax paid by Christians everywhere to the Pope. During that time he found favour and patronage from Henry VII and was granted the bishopric of Bath and Wells in 1504. He then became Henry's representative at the papal court in Rome, where he remained, becoming a cardinal. He is said only to have been to Wells twice (July 1510 and February 1513) and neither time did he stay very long, instead leaving his onerous duties to a deputy or vicar-general. A later Italian

collector of Peter's Pence who also came to Wells, Polydore Vergil, was already a celebrity throughout Europe. Vergil was a humanist scholar of renown who had already written two books and was immediately sought out by the great scholars of the time including Thomas More. Possibly at More's instigation he started to write his *Anglicae Historiae*, the first full-scale history of England from earliest times to his own day. This was a work of great scholarship and unlike the monkish chroniclers who had gone before him, who were more storytellers than historians, he went back to original sources to discover what had really happened. Rather sensibly, the book also makes great play of the Tudor family lineage and the strength of their claim to the throne, a matter of great sensitivity for the king. Henry VII was delighted and appointed Vergil to the archdeaconry of Wells in 1508. Although the new archdeacon spent much of his time in London, he did also do his duty in Wells, saying that he benefitted morally himself from having to set a good example. On the eve of the Reformation, Vergil described the canons of Wells as "men of honest behaviour and well-learned."

TOP LEFT: Opening page of Pliny's Natural History.

TOP RIGHT: Polydore Vergil.

LEFT: Title page of Vergil's English History.

REFORMATION, WAR AND REBELLION

No part of the English church was left untouched by the upheaval known as the Reformation. Refused a divorce by the pope, Henry VIII split from Rome, systematically stripping the monasteries of wealth, land and power. Half England's cathedrals were monastic and with the Dissolution of the Monasteries, had to be re-founded. Not a monastic institution Wells was spared the worst but did not escape entirely. By act of Parliament, chantries were abolished and masses no longer said for the dead. The new Protestant religion put its emphasis on the living and their understanding of the bible which they could now read in English rather than Latin. The two chapels at the end of the nave were part of the fabric and could not be demolished, but the new pulpit springing from the wall of Sugar's chantry, installed by the first Protestant bishop, William Knight, shows the new emphasis on preaching, as sermons were introduced for the first time and became central to worship. The Lady Chapel in the Cloister rebuilt by Bishop Stillington [1466-91] as a mortuary chapel for himself was stripped and demolished (the foundations can still be seen in the Camery garden). The confiscation of chantry incomes led to severe financial hardship and the canons were forced to sell off the metal canopies over the tombs of their predecessors and many of their brass effigies. The hollows where they once lay on the floor of the nave can still be seen. In addition all the elaborate and glorious medieval wall paintings depicting the saints and telling biblical stories for an illiterate congregation were whitewashed over.

As Henry VIII's reforms began, the Chapter recognised their perilous position and tried to protect themselves by electing the arch reformer and the king's chief minister Thomas Cromwell, as dean in 1537. Cromwell saw many of the Cathedral's treasures as being overtly Catholic and he shipped them and the contents of the library to London to be turned into hard cash. It would be another century before the book collection was rebuilt. After Henry's death and the accession to the throne of his reforming Protestant son, Edward VI, life changed substantially for the canons and vicars choral of the Cathedral. The number of services was drastically reduced and the canons had to learn how to write and deliver sermons. A law was passed for the abolition of chantries in 1547. This brought financial hardship since much of the income they had provided now went to the Crown. Former chantry priests could not be turned

The Chain Library

out on to the street and had to be supported until new employment could be found in parishes. One of the biggest changes of the Reformation was that the clergy were permitted to marry. The first married bishop was William Barlow [1548-1553], who found it very difficult to support his wife and seven children. His predecessor had surrendered some of the episcopal estates to Thomas Cromwell, but now the Crown and King Edward's uncle, the duke of Somerset, deprived the bishopric of most of its land. The duke wanted estates in the county from whence he derived his title and the bishop was the easiest source. His final humiliation came when Somerset turned him out of the palace in 1550. Needing a home, the bishop in turn took possession of the deanery, much to the discomfort of the dean. When Edward's Catholic sister Mary came to the throne the old religion was restored for a few years before the Anglican Church emerged under Elizabeth. Luckily the queen recognised that while she

LEFT: Sugar's chantry with the pulpit built into it.

ABOVE RIGHT: Archbishop Thomas Cranmer's handwriting.

might disapprove of married clergy, she would have to tolerate them, while her love of music rescued cathedrals from the doldrums and led to a magnificent flowering of church music under composers such as Tallis and Byrd.

The affairs of the Church stabilised under Queen Elizabeth. At Wells, the number of canons was reduced and the Cathedral was managed by a small group of them who lived on site. With the abolition of all the masses for the dead, the daily services were far fewer and that also meant a cut in the number of vicars choral. A new charter for their College limited their number to fourteen; however the good news was that now they could marry. The number of boy choristers remained the same and occasionally the best of them was sent from Wells to London to serve in the Chapel Royal. John Pitcher was one such boy. A letter in the Wells archive from Queen Elizabeth explains that after six years of royal service his voice "begynneth to change" and he had become "not so fitte

for our service." The letter requests Wells to take him back as a "singeing man" or vicar choral, thus effectively giving him a house and a job for life. It seems they had no great desire to take him, and hoped that if they ignored the request the Queen would forget all about it. However, this was Elizabeth's second letter on the subject making it clear that she felt her inquiry was not being given due consideration and that the authorities at Wells might think carefully before disregarding a second royal plea. As it happened, the boy did not come back, suggesting he was conveniently found another posting elsewhere, where he would not have to be fed and clothed by sovereign or Cathedral.

The impact of the English Civil War in the mid 17th century was far more catastrophic at Wells than ever the Reformation had been. Initially held for King Charles, the town was eventually taken and occupied by the forces of Parliament. To understand the Civil War it is vital to see it as a struggle not only for power but for men's souls. Some of the Puritan ultra-extremists of the Parliamentary side had little in common with the modern Church of England. They considered the king to be in the spiritual grip of his French Catholic wife. Their marriage was a political expedient to cement an alliance against Spain. It was the first time a Protestant prince had married a Catholic princess and had even required a special dispensation from the pope for it to be permitted. As the country deteriorated into civil war, Puritans, who considered stained glass and statues depicting saints as well as church organs fundamentally contrary to true religion, took the opportunity at Wells to smash whatever they considered offensive which was within reach. Some of the broken glass was secretly preserved and later used to create crazy-paving style windows in the Lady Chapel. Thankfully, the wonderful Jesse window above the high altar survived, almost certainly because it was too high up to get at. The organ was virtually new having been installed in about 1620.

ABOVE: Angels atop the modern organ.

The initial vandalism suffered by the Cathedral during the war was merely a foretaste of the disasters yet to befall Wells. After the Parliamentary side were victorious and Oliver Cromwell was set at the head of the new Commonwealth, official religious attitudes hardened still further. In 1645 bishoprics were abolished and cathedrals were closed throughout the country. In Wells the canons dispersed and lay low, and the dean, Walter Raleigh,

(nephew of the great Elizabethan explorer of that name) was imprisoned. His home had already been ransacked, his cattle driven away and his wife and children thrown onto the street by the time he was forced to give himself up to Parliamentary forces at Bridgwater. He was moved from prison to prison before finally being brought back to suffer the indignity of confinement in his own deanery, then under the control of a local shoemaker called David Barrett. Barrett was charged with keeping an eye on the known Royalist sympathiser, and it is believed Raleigh's death came as a result of a scuffle between them when the cobbler wanted to see the contents of a letter written by the dean to his wife. He died from stab wounds and was buried secretly at night under the dean's seat in the quire; the place is marked by a plaque. Francis Standish, the vicar choral who buried him, was briefly imprisoned for it. On the Restoration of Charles II in 1660, the cathedrals were reopened after fifteen years of darkness and Bishop Piers returned to his palace. Robert Creyghton, who had been Charles's chaplain in exile, was made dean. However, on arrival at the deanery he found that it was already occupied by the Puritan preacher, Cornelius Burges. Burges flatly refused to leave and Creyghton had to go to law to have

RIGHT: Bishop Creyghton's
brass lectern.

FAR RIGHT: Bishop Ken
(1637-1711).

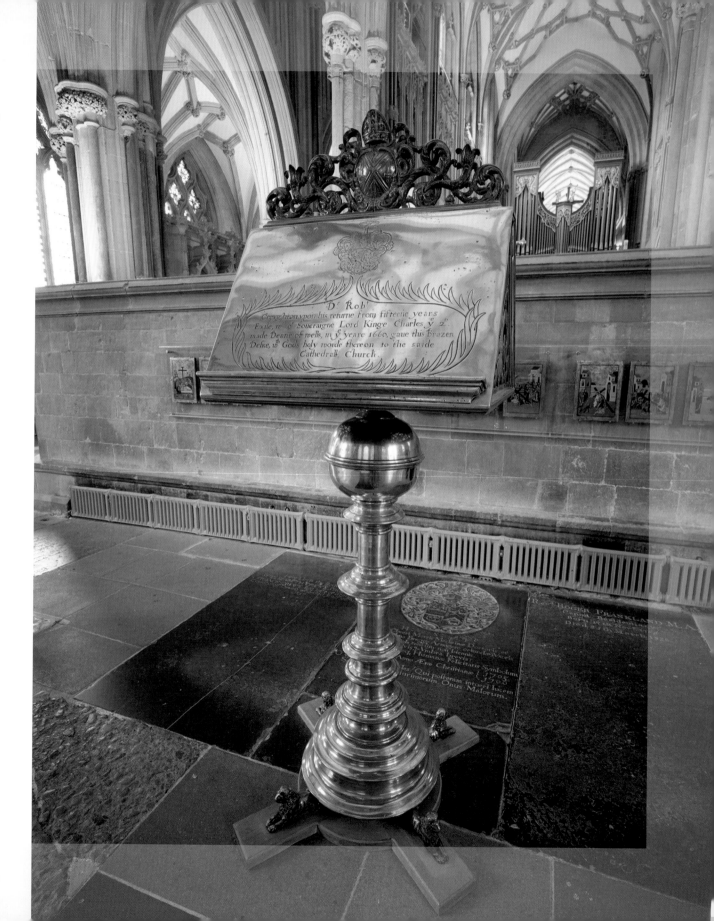

him thrown out. A year earlier, Burges is understood to have been offered the princely sum of £12,000 for the house. He had made a sizeable fortune buying up alienated church lands and had rebuilt the deanery in fine style, moving in in 1649. He is also accused of stripping the lead from the Cathedral to pay for the work. As it was he lost virtually everything and is reputed near the end of his life to have sold much of his library to buy sufficient bread to survive. Creyghton did not live in the deanery for long. When Bishop Piers died Creyghton took his place, the only dean at Wells ever to become bishop. The great brass lectern which now stands in the retroquire was the gift of Bishop Creyghton. Although the badly damaged organ was initially patched up, a completely new one was ordered from Robert Taunton of Bristol in 1662 at a cost of £800.

The most revered of all Wells bishops was the saintly Thomas Ken (1685-91). There is a long tradition in the Church of clerics, great and small, standing up to royal authority. Thomas Ken stood up to no less than three kings. Ken was brought up by his half-sister Anne and her husband Izaak Walton, author of the famous, The Compleat Angler. He was a scholar, musician and man of prayer, but is probably best known as a writer of hymns, some of which, including *Awake, my soul, and with the sun*, are still in use today. In 1683, while a canon at Winchester, he refused to permit Charles II's mistress, Nell Gwyn, to lodge at his house during a royal visit. Charles wisely knew which battles were worth fighting and respected Ken's decision, leaving Nell to find other arrangements. When the bishopric of Bath and Wells fell vacant, the king allegedly declared "Odd's fish! Who shall have Bath and Wells but the little fellow who would not give poor Nelly a lodging?" Ken was consecrated in 1685 and just a few weeks later one of his first official duties was to attend the king on his death bed. Yet again Ken shoed away the latest mistress and demanded the queen be sent for to be with her husband at the end. Charles II was succeeded by his brother James II who was blessed with none of his brother's intellect, emotional stability or good sense, but above all he was a Catholic. James wanted to ease the restrictions on his fellow Catholics and people feared he wanted to restore the country to the Roman faith. Within weeks of his taking the throne a rebellion broke out, begun in Somerset by the duke of Monmouth, Charles II's illegitimate but Protestant, son. Wells was caught in the thick of the chaos. Rebels occupied the Cathedral, damaging anything they regarded as being too Catholic. However they were crushed by royal troops at the battle of Sedgemoor less than twenty miles from Wells. Many of those who survived, possibly hundreds of them, were taken back to Wells and held prisoner in various places around the city, including the cloisters. Conditions were appalling. The smell emanating from this dirty and dispirited mass of beaten men was so awful that no one could work in the Library above the east cloister for more than half an hour at a time. The prisoners were put on trial before the notoriously cruel Judge Jefferies at what came to be known as the Bloody Assizes. Travelling across the country to towns where rebels were held, Jeffries tried more than 1,400 rebels finding the vast majority of them guilty. Sentences included burning and being hanged, drawn and quartered. Ken had been in London at the time of the battle but hurried back to plead for leniency. He visited the condemned men regularly and appealed directly to the king for mercy. Certainly due in part to Ken's interventions only three hundred executions were carried out, the bodies of the guilty put on display around the country as a warning to others who might consider taking up arms against their anointed king. About nine hundred other rebels were transported to the West Indies effectively to work as slaves on plantations. Monmouth was taken to London

and publicly beheaded for his crimes. Right up to the moment the axe fell, Ken was there with him to offer spiritual comfort.

James II learnt no lessons from the Monmouth Rebellion and continued with his plans to redress the balance for Catholics. He issued a new law called the Declaration of Indulgence which we might read today as quite liberal and humane but which was seen in 1687 as dangerous and inflammatory. It called for the removal of legal demands that everyone should worship in the Church of England and for Catholics to be allowed to take public office. Ken was one of seven bishops who openly opposed the Declaration and he was thrown in the Tower of London and put on trial, although eventually acquitted. After such experiences it might be reasonable to expect Ken to toe the line from then on. James II was deposed and replaced with the steadfastly Protestant William III. The two men had met before; Ken had been chaplain to William's queen, Mary (daughter of James II), years

earlier. Yet once again, Ken's conscience got in the way of his personal safety. He had sworn an oath of allegiance to James II who was still alive if in exile. He felt he could not swear a new oath to a new king without breaking the one, just as sacred, he had already made. Ken was removed from office and never reinstated, but Wells was clearly still in his mind; he left many of his books to the Cathedral Library where still they reside today. He was much loved for his kindness, humanity and generosity to the poor.

It is very rarely a good career move to follow in the footsteps of someone who is much loved and in this way it is hard not to feel sorry for Richard Kidder. A perfectly kind, decent and inoffensive man his mistake was to be put in as bishop while Ken still lived. Kidder, was never popular, and even the saintly Ken referred to him, rather bitterly, as "my successor or rather supplanter." Kidder's

fate was as dramatic as it was undeserved. He and his wife were killed in their bed when a pair of chimneys crashed through the roof of the bishop's palace during the Great Storm of 1703. Kidder's fate was unfortunate but far from unique. Possibly 15,000 people lost their lives at land and sea during the two day disaster. Wells does not have a large number of grand memorials, but near the door to the Chapter House steps is one to Bishop Kidder, erected by his grieving daughter. This lady clearly felt that if she was paying for it she would have her money's worth, and her recumbent figure takes a highly prominent position on the memorial. To the right of the Kidder memorial is one to an earlier bishop, John Still [1593-1608]. Still, who was a very able scholar, was also an excellent preacher, an ability greatly prized in the early Church of England. This won him rapid promotion both at Cambridge and in the church. He was the first married master of St John's College, Cambridge, and had ten children, seven of whom survived to be frequent

parents themselves. Their descendants are now scattered round the world, many of them in the United States and the Cathedral receives frequent inquiries from them about their genealogical connections. Despite having sympathy with the hard-line puritans of East Anglia, Still was a strong defender of the Elizabethan settlement of the Anglican Church, which brought him his bishopric. Incongruously, rumours persist that he may have been the author of a noisy slapstick comedy which was hugely popular at the time, published anonymously and called, *Gammer Gurton's Needle*.

LEFT: The ceiling of the Nave.

ABOVE: Memorial to the unlucky Bishop Kidder.

RIGHT: Memorial to Bishop Still, a man of many descendants.

CALM AFTER THE STORM

The reign of William III effectively marked the end of major religious upheavals in England. The 18th century in Wells, as in so many other cathedral cities, was a time of relative prosperity and of a growing middle class. The Cathedral settled into rather comfortable stagnation. At the beginning of the century, Daniel Defoe, writer of Robinson Crusoe, described it after a visit as a place where the clergy "live very handsomely" and that in Wells "there is no want of

good company." The canons were well educated, well paid and far from over-worked. Many came from well-connected families. They married among themselves and nominated their children and nephews to be new canons as positions became available, sometimes creating entire dynasties which rarely moved more than a few hundred yards from the Cathedral walls. This cosy comfort was not without its advantages for the Cathedral itself. The fabric was looked after well; roof timbers were repaired, new galleries built above the quire stalls and seating provided for town dignitaries between the stalls and the high altar. Successive bishops were learned, wise and good to the poor, but looking back through history there is a quiet sense of drift as the 18th century morphed into the 19th. All around great social and national change was taking place, but the industrial revolution, the rise of Methodism and the wars with Napoleon's post-Revolutionary France seem hardly to have disturbed the tranquillity of the Cathedral and its people. There were advantages to be had from French misfortune; huge quantities of stained glass were looted from French churches during the revolution, and canny English dealers bought up job lots to sell to churches in England either for new build, or to fill in the gaps created during the Reformation and Civil War periods. In 1813 the Cathedral took advantage of one such bargain buy to replace sections of the west window badly damaged in the Great Storm which had killed Bishop Kidder in 1703. One of the best French Renaissance pieces, probably from a church in Rouen

LEFT: The Quire as it is today.

French glass – the beheading of
John the Baptist.

RIGHT: St John the Evangelist
and his eagle.

and dating from 1507, shows the execution of John the Baptist; it is now high up on the east wall of the north transept. In St Katherine's Chapel scenes from the life of St John the Evangelist, are also considered to have come from Rouen.

Dean Edmund Goodenough (1831-1845) put an end to this torpor beginning a major programme of restoration and modernisation. He was largely responsible for the uncluttered look of the Cathedral today moving most of the monuments to the cloisters. He also began the "Great Scrape," cleaning centuries of whitewash from the walls. Sadly this zealous process also led to the removal of the medieval wall paintings which had been hidden beneath the whitewash since the Reformation. In the quire, the galleries which had been built over the stalls to provide extra seating were removed and new stalls placed further back within the line of the arches. Goodenough was in his element at Wells and seems to have found happiness there after a somewhat troubled life. He had previously been appointed headmaster of Westminster school, which was in a sorry state. Many of the buildings were falling down but Goodenough failed to convince the school authorities

to pay for improvements. Discipline among the boys was virtually non-existent. A kind man, Goodenough tried to make a stand. In 1819 he broke with custom and flogged a sixth-former for being drunk. There was uproar and he was forced to back down. Shortly afterwards he tried to introduce new rules limiting the responsibilities of the younger boys who slaved as fags for their elders. He said they should no longer have to black shoes or clean candlesticks. The boys rose up in riot, an event known as the "shoe-and-candlestick rebellion." Admiral Lord Paget, a pupil at the school at the time wrote in his autobiography, "At the usual hour the head-master, followed, as was customary, by the second master, and the six ushers of forms, and attended by the king's scholars, marched up the hall. At a given signal, all the upper boys were to commence firing their books at his head, and the fags were to supply ammunition." During his period in charge of the school, numbers fell steadily and he was forced to resign in August 1828. While he had many of his own, it was another incident involving children which led to his death. Goodenough saw some boys trespassing in a field near his home and tried to chase them off. He collapsed in a fit and died.

Goodenough's successor, Richard Jenkyns (1845-1854) continued his restoration and funded much of the work in the quire personally. Dean Edward Plumptre (1881-1891) initiated services for the people of Wells, carol services, harvest festivals, choral festivals, setting up an altar in the nave when the congregations became too large to fit into the quire. His introduction of white altar cloths and jewelled candlesticks did not please everyone, but instituting regular holidays for the choristers went down very well with them. The Oxford Dictionary of National Biography says of his tenure, "He was an ideal dean, possessing a genuine talent for business, and being always ready to consider the suggestions of others. Not only the Cathedral and the theological college but the city of Wells, its hospital, its almshouse, and its workhouse, commanded his service." Plumptre was the author of a number of successful hymns and is regarded by many as one of the Church of England's greatest authors of sacred poetry.

The transformation of the Cathedral's appearance continued into the 20th century. Much of the stained glass admired by visitors was added in the last decade of the 19th century and the first of the 20th. Animals and birds had been images popular in the Middle Ages, then after a long gap, more modern artists followed suit. The Victorians often included the symbols of saints they depicted, so St John the Baptist has his lamb and Saint Mark his lion. The most modern examples are the carved symbols of the Four Evangelists outside the North Porch. Again, like their medieval forebears, Victorian artists loved including angels in their work and walking round the Cathedral spotting where angels appear in glass or carvings can become addictive. The most spectacular of the modern windows, the large ones in the North and South Transepts were both made by James Powell and Sons and installed in 1903 and 1905 respectively. Powells was the oldest and most successful glass-making business in the country. The company's research in the late 19th century into methods for producing new colours made advances which made possible the invention of the light bulb and X-Ray tubes. The south transept window illustrates the River of Life, seen at the top of the window, with St John in a red cloak, St Peter in a blue one and St Paul in a green one. In the north transept the wall of glass is part of the memorial to men who died in the Boer War and is full of images of warriors, among them King David, Henry V, the Duke of Wellington and General Gordon (the hero of Khartoum). In 1926 the French Renaissance glass was removed from the great west window and the panels put elsewhere; in its place a new centre panel for the window was made by another celebrated glass painter, Archibald Nicholson.

A CATHEDRAL FOR THE MODERN AGE

One of the biggest puzzles for new visitors to Wells is picking out the new from the old. We have seen how the Scissor Arches are often mistaken for modern innovation. Above them stands the Rood incorporating the figures of the Crucified Christ flanked by the Virgin and St John. These look medieval but are in fact modern. Similar figures were placed there in the 15th century, possibly to replace earlier ones, by the Treasurer, Hugh Sugar, whose chantry chapel in the Nave is the pair to that of Bishop Bubwith. These figures were destroyed at the Reformation and for centuries nothing took their place. In 1920 a plain cross was placed there by Dean Armitage Robinson. It was an experiment, with considerable fear that many in the diocese would find it too Roman Catholic. In the event opposition was overcome and three new figures were carved by Guglielmo Tosi. His original model for the Rood now serves as an altar piece in St Calixtus' Chapel.

In the Middle Ages the Cathedral would have been full of altars where priests regularly said masses for the dead. Only the rich could afford to commission the building of separate chantry

ABOVE: The altarpiece of St Martin's Chapel.

RIGHT: The Rood above the Scissor Arches.

chapels, but it was three of these which physically survived the abolition of chantries and are once again used as chapels. Now Wells has fewer side chapels than many cathedrals, only nine, excluding the Lady Chapel. Some like the chantry chapels in the Nave, and St Stephen's or the Mothers' Union chapel have very simple altarpieces; others are much more elaborate and all are relatively modern. That in the chapel of Corpus Christi, off the North Quire Aisle, is medieval but was moved from the East Cloister in 1866 by George Kibble and the colouring restored in 1975. The two adjoining chapels of St. Katherine and St. John the Baptist in the South Quire Aisle both have altarpieces or reredos composed of fragments of late perpendicular wooden tracery. These were reused to form the front of the galleries erected above the stalls in the quire to accommodate the wives of canons after the Reformation. The fragments were reassembled in the early 20th century by Sir Charles Nicholson, the Cathedral architect and brother to Archibald whose glass is in the west window. The centrepiece of that in St. Katherine's is a fine piece of late 17th century Flemish carving, the provenance of which is unknown. Nicholson also designed the elaborate carved and painted altarpiece in St Martin's Chapel in the South Transept. Like the altarpiece in the adjoining chapel of St. Calixtus, it was carved by Gugliemo Tosi.

St Stephen's Chapel is the Mothers' Union chapel, divided off from the retroquire by a colourful screen. This looks as if it is made from metal but is actually wooden. It, together with all the furniture in the chapel, the altar screens and the

The medieval masons' tracing floor high above the North Porch.

banner, were designed by Sir Ninian Comper in 1935 and paid for in instalments by the Mothers' Union. Comper was the leading ecclesiastic architect of his day, an Anglo-Catholic who designed for Anglican and Roman Catholic churches and convents alike including Westminster Abbey. He was particularly noted as a designer of vestments, banners and windows, showing an understanding of the liturgy far in advance of any of his contemporary architects. The wooden screen dividing this chapel from the neighbouring Corpus Christi Chapel is unusual in that it had previously been used to form cow stalls although its original purpose is unknown. The screen came from a house near Glastonbury as a gift to the Cathedral in 1927. Inside the chapel are the only surviving fourteenth century floor tiles in the Cathedral.

Very unusually, the city of Wells has no war memorial. Men of the Somerset Light Infantry who died in the Boer War are commemorated on the north wall of the North Transept. After World War One, Dean Armitage Robinson persuaded the County War Memorial Committee to abandon the idea of a cross on the Cathedral green and instead fund the refurbishment of the two chapels of St Martin (a Roman soldier) and St Calixtus in the South Transept. The chapels were dedicated as the Somerset War Memorial on St Andrew's Day, 1922, in the presence of the duke of York, the future King George VI. The Book of Remembrance, containing the names of the men and women of Somerset who fell in both world wars, is housed in St Martin's Chapel. In 2009 the Cathedral was the setting for the memorial service of Harry Patch, who died aged 111. He was the last "fighting Tommy," who had served in the trenches and spent his last years in Wells. A memorial to him is situated outside Wells Museum, just to the north of the Cathedral. If the visitor looks up at the wording above the entrance to these chapels, it reads, Remember the Men of Somerset who in the cause of freedom died for God and Country 1914-1918 and 1939-1945. Rather eerily, the reference to the Second War was added with great ease as for some unknown reason the original sign writer had left sufficient space for its inclusion. The chapel of St Calixtus is reserved for private prayer.

Only in the 20th century did the Cathedral begin to approach the colourfulness of the middle ages. The plainness of the Nave is broken only by the beautiful flower arrangements and the altar frontal, but on entering the Quire the visitor is presented with a dazzling display of colour, not only from the great east window, but also from the embroideries. The needlework of the quire was the brainchild of Dean Richard Malden [1933-50] who had seen service as a chaplain on board Royal Navy ships in the First World War and was also the successful author of ghost stories. The needlework was almost wholly designed by Alice, Lady Hylton, and

executed by ladies and a few men of the diocese between 1937 and 1952, with financial support from the newly-established Friends of Wells Cathedral. The hangings of the stalls comprise the arms of all the bishops interspersed with special decorative designs for the stalls of the dignitaries. The hangings were later followed by embroidered seat cushions for the stalls and elsewhere in the Quire. The striking modern altar frontals for the Quire and Nave, which are changed according to the season of the church year, date from 1999 and were designed by Jane Lemon and Maurice Strike. The quire frontals were made by the Royal School of Needlework and those for the nave altar by the Sarum Group at Salisbury.

Only during Lent do the plain walls of the Nave become colourful. Visitors are likely to have their eyes drawn to the striking Stations of the Cross. These icons are a series of artistic representations of various scenes as Christ carried

ABOVE : The beautifully painted wooden screen of St Stephen's Chapel.

RIGHT: St Stephen's Chapel.

the cross to his crucifixion. The usual number of scenes now is fourteen, ending with his body being laid in the tomb. Icons are holy pictures in the tradition of the Eastern Orthodox Church. Painted as aids to prayer, they follow strict rules of form and composition, unchanged over the centuries. At other times of the year the icons are on display in the retroquire. They were painted in the year 2000 as a millennium project by Bulgarian Sylvia Demitrova, when she was artist-in-residence at the Cathedral for a year. She and her husband, Simon Potter, were actually married in the Cathedral. Her works can also be seen in the chapel of the Bishop's Palace and at Downside Abbey. The icon of St Andrew, the Cathedral's patron saint, which stands at the entrance to the south quire aisle, was commissioned by the Chapter in 1999 and is the work of Aliksandre Gormatiouk of Moscow.

Under Dean Patrick Mitchell (1973-1989) major archaeological work was undertaken in the Camery garden which added greatly to our knowledge and understanding of the early history of this holy site. It is, however, his great campaign for the restoration of the West Front for which Dean Patrick will be remembered. Other restoration work had been carried out when necessary, including a full-scale effort in 1871-4, but a century later another was due. Begun in 1975, this was able to employ modern scientific methods and revealed evidence of the paint which had once covered the statues. The statue of the Risen Christ in the topmost gable had long been damaged beyond repair, and the Friends of Wells Cathedral paid for a new interpretation by the sculptor David Wynne. This was put in place in 1984. Dean Patrick's wife Mary died in 1986 and in her memory a garden was planted in front of the West Cloister. With the development of the new Entry Cloister in 2009, the garden was remodelled and replanted to give enjoyment to all who visit the Cathedral.

One of the main tasks for Cathedral authorities is the preservation and occasionally restoration of its stonework. In the Interpretation Centre are displayed a set of modern stonemason's tools which would be instantly recognisable to his medieval counterpart. For

LEFT: Former cow stalls are now the screen for Corpus Christi Chapel.

ABOVE: A delicately embroidered Quire Seat.

BELOW: Remembrance.

much of the 19th century any necessary work was contracted out, but more recently a mason has been part of the permanent staff. A photograph of 1925 shows one of the masons who had climbed out beyond the scaffold to test the finial of one of the great buttresses and found that a large chunk of it came off in his hand. One of the Cathedral's great unsung heroes is Bert Wheeler, who was first master mason and then clerk of works between 1935 and 1978, having already served as a chorister. For decades his feeling for the local Doulting stone of which the Cathedral is built dictated his policy of careful stone replacement, which has ensured that Wells has not been totally refaced like many other old churches. His aim when the great repair of the West Front began was to "conserve the concept," keeping the whole religious and theological vision of its builders intact and repairing and replacing only that which was strictly necessary. Wheeler claimed his love affair with the Cathedral began as a small boy when he crawled into a gap in the masonry to see how the wall looked inside. His successor as master mason was David Rice, immortalised in stone on the south-east corner of the Chapter House.

All things change and the Cathedral at Wells is no exception. Although we think of the building as having been completed eight hundred years ago alterations are forever taking place, but always with the intention of blending new and old in harmony. The most significant building project since the 14th century was completed in 2009 with the addition of greatly improved facilities for visitors. This involved opening up a medieval doorway into the West Cloister from the newly-built Entry

Cloister which also houses the shop and restaurant. The great wooden doors, always open to visitors, can be easily missed by those passing through them, but are worth a moment or two to admire the modern craftsmanship which matches them to their older counterparts. The doorway at the end of the East Cloister, leading to the new public toilets and to the new Education and Music building is likewise a former medieval doorway with new doors. The new Education Room is modelled on a medieval hall, with a timber-framed roof space. Its windows on to the Camery garden allow visitors to look in and admire.

What will the future hold for the Cathedral? It has withstood enormous religious and political upheavals, enduring neglect sometimes and a destructive over-enthusiasm at others. Importantly, what remains would still be entirely recognisable, in parts at least, to Reginald de Bohun or Adam Lock. The project they began was realised. It is a place of worship, of tranquillity and of glorious musicality, just as it was meant to be. A constant witness to history but above all to the Glory of God, always changing, always the same, it is built not just from stone and glass, but from the blood, sweat, toil and tears of those whose lives go to make up its true story.

ABOVE: The Cathedral's patron saint, Andrew.

RIGHT: A head for heights and a surprising handful of stone (1925).

FAR RIGHT: The new doors of Pilgrims' Porch.